Where Are You From?

Seed Learning

Where are you from?

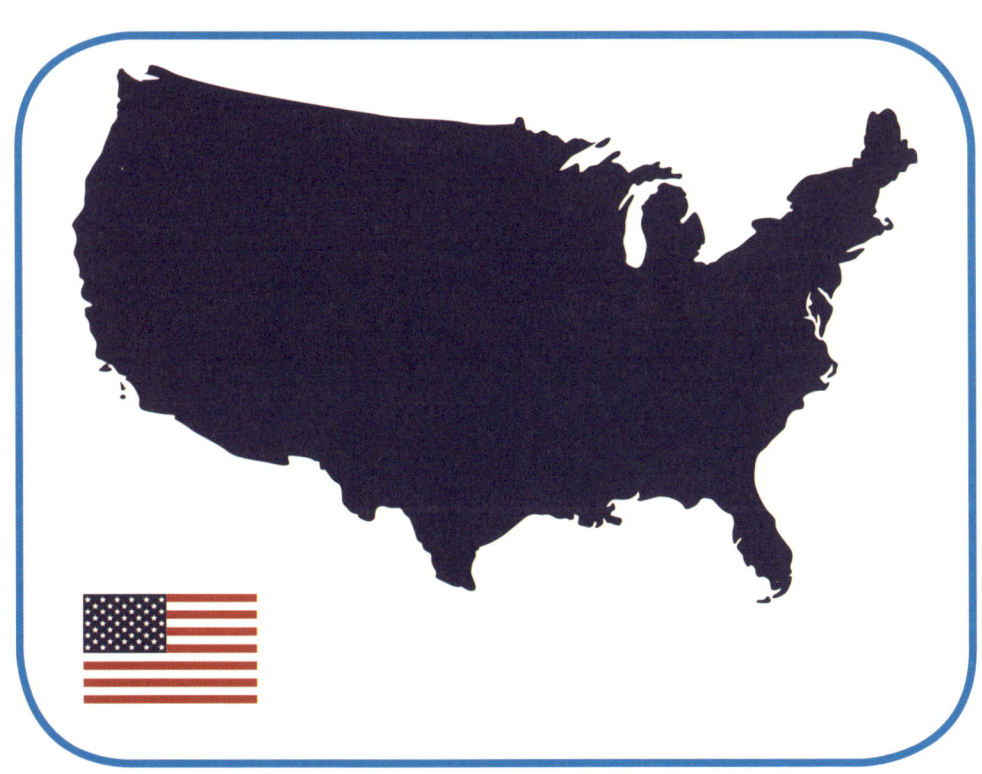

America.

I'm from America.

Where are you from?

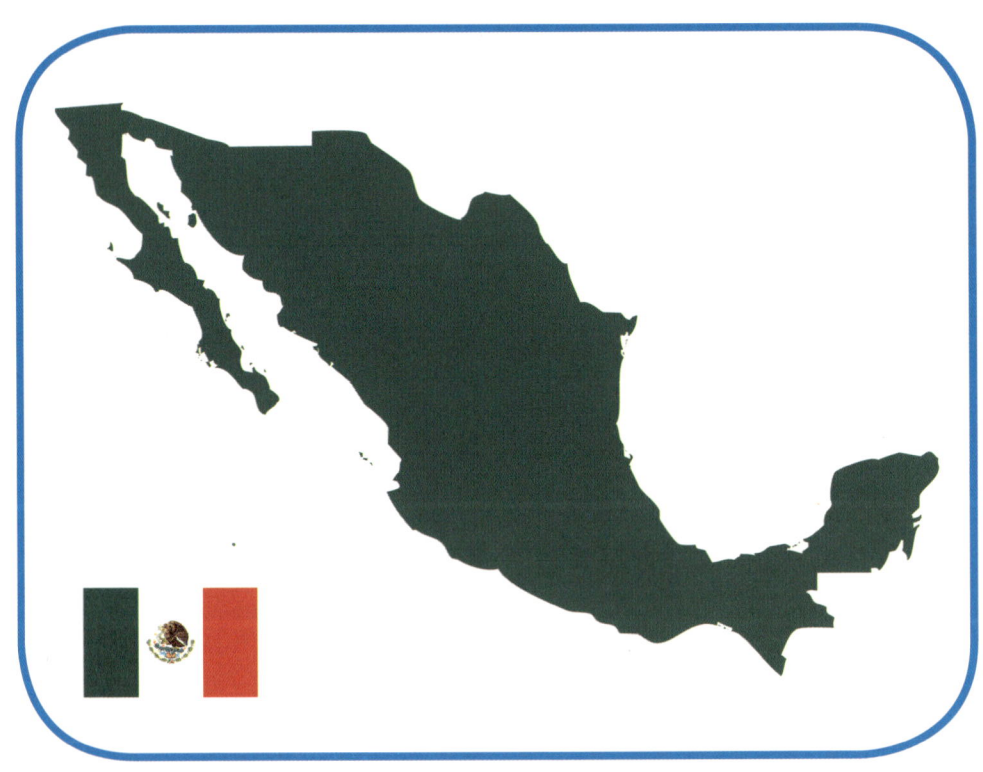

Mexico.

I'm from Mexico.

Where are you from?

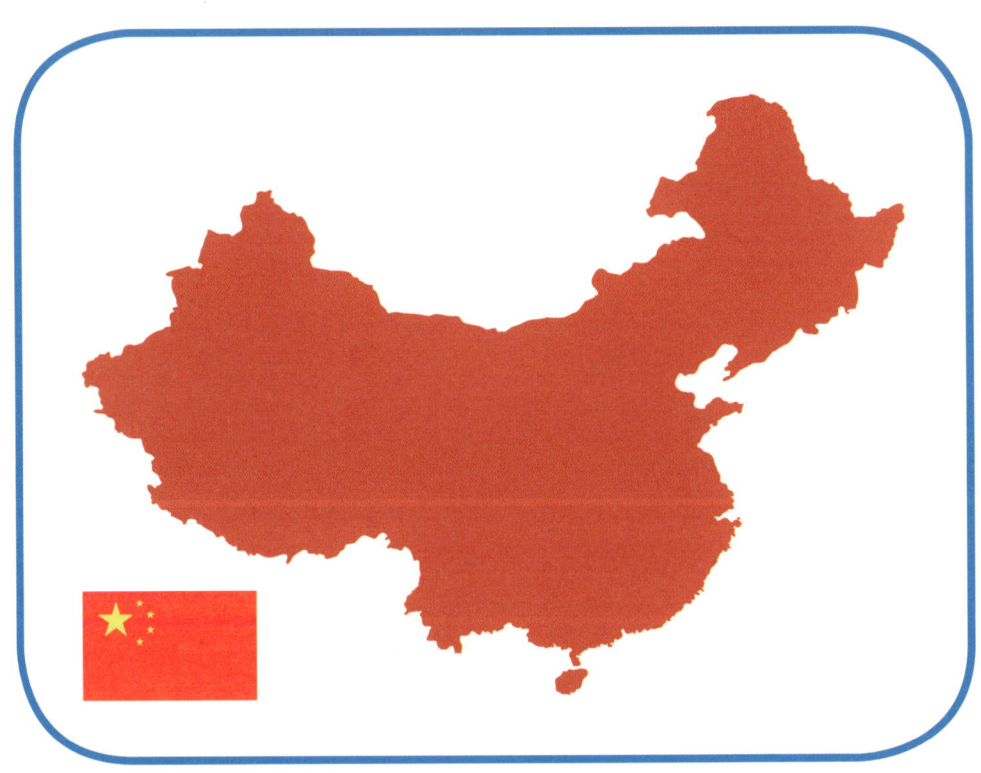

China.

I'm from China.

Where are you from?

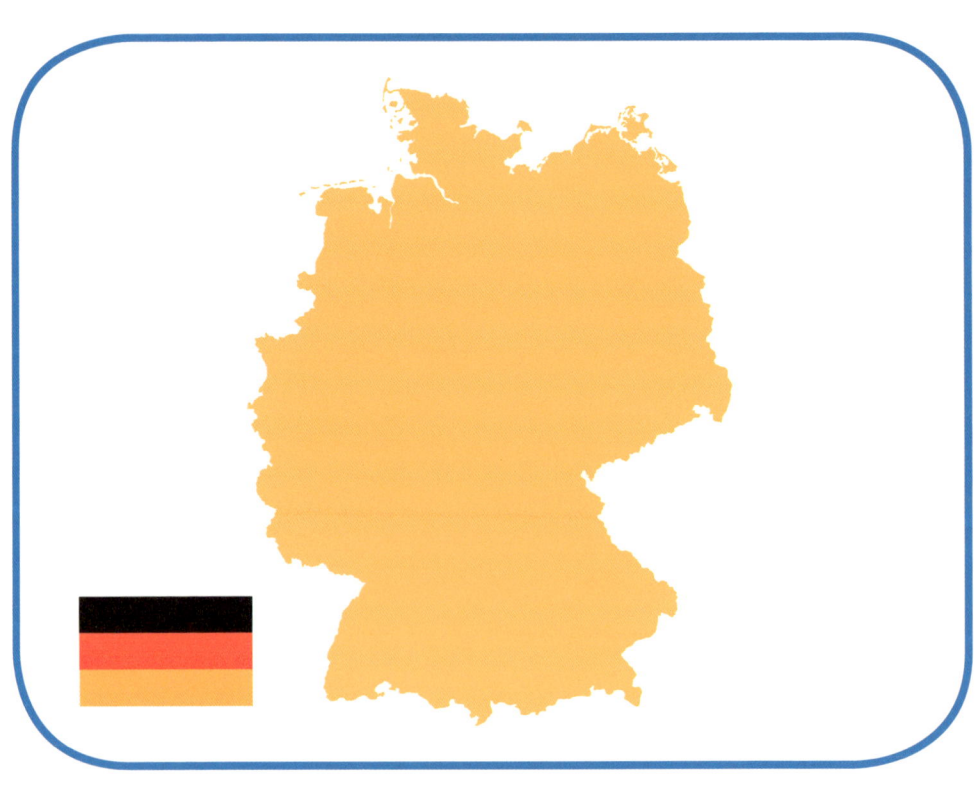

Germany.

I'm from Germany.

Where are you from?

Turkey.

I'm from Turkey.

Where are you from?

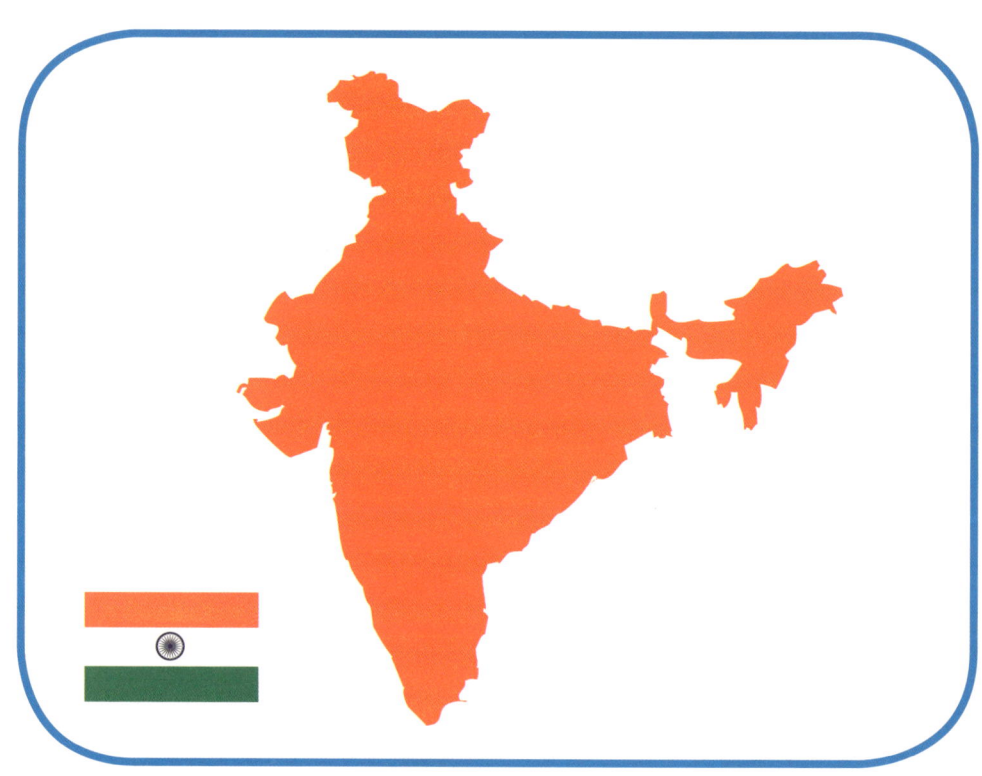

India.

I'm from India.

Where are you from?

Russia.

I'm from Russia.

Let's learn about Yom Kippur.

September

Sunday	Monday	Tuesday	Wednesday	Thursday	Friday	Saturday
		1	2	3	4	5
6	7	8	9	10	11	12
13	14	15	16	17	18	19
20	21	22	23	24	25	26
27	28	29	30			

Trace the word September and circle the date.